The Release of Nelson Mandela

11 February 1990

CHERRYTREE BOOKS

A Cherrytree Book

This edition published in 2008
by Cherrytree Books, part of
The Evans Publishing Group
2A Portman Mansions
Chiltern Street
London WIU 6NR

British Library Cataloguing in Publication Data
Malam, John.
  The release of Nelson Mandela. - (Dates with history)
  1.Mandela, Nelson, 1918- - Imprisonment
  2.South Africa - History - 1961- - Juvenile literature
  I.Title
  968'.064

ISBN 9781842345375

To contact the author, send an email to:
johnmalam@aol.com

Picture credits:

Bailey's African History Archives: 13, 18
Corbis: 7, 23, 25, 26
Hodder Wayland Picture Library: 8, 15
Hulton Getty: 20
Link Picture Library: 9, 10, 19, 22
McGregor Museum, Duggan-Cronin Collection: 11
Rex Features: 17
Topham Picturepoint: 12, 14, 16, 21, 24, 27

Printed in China by WKT Co. Ltd

Contents

His name is 'Troublemaker'

Among the rolling hills and fields of the **Transkei** region of South Africa are the villages of the **Thembu** people. This is their ancient homeland, where they have lived for centuries, farming the land and raising livestock. The village of Mvezo stands on a hill, from where there are magnificent views across the nearby River Mbashe. Mvezo is similar to many villages in the area, but it has a great and proud claim to fame.

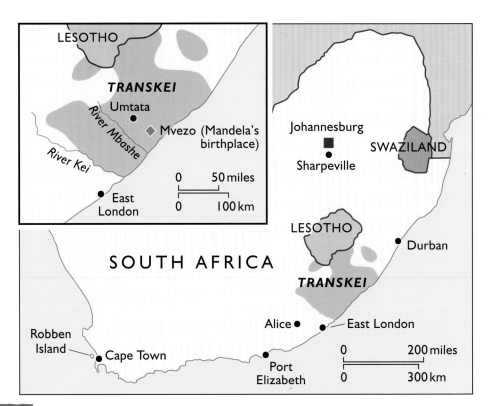

A map of South Africa showing the Transkei region.

On 18 July 1918, a boy was born in Mvezo, in a simple hut with a thatched roof. The boy's parents, Henry and Nosekeni Mandela, called their son Rolihlahla, which means 'pulling the branch of a tree'. It can also mean 'troublemaker', which was a good name to give to the boy, though no one knew that at the time.

Rolihlahla was one of thirteen children. His father was the headman of Mvezo village and advisor to the Thembu king. Rolihlahla's great-grandfather himself had been a Thembu king. When Rolihlahla was very young the Mandela family moved to Qunu, a nearby village. It was here that Rolihlahla spent his boyhood.

The story of how Rolihlahla Mandela, an African boy from the Transkei, became one of the world's greatest leaders, is also the story of South Africa and its troubled history.

A modern-day village in the Transkei region of South Africa.

Africa is for Africans

Rolihlahla Mandela was born at an important time in the history of Africa. The early years of the 1900s saw the beginning of a new form of politics amongst African nations. It was a political movement known as **nationalism**, which is when nations believe they should be free to rule themselves.

South Africa had many diamond mines, and dealers from Europe set up businesses there to buy and sell diamonds.

However, at this time, much of Africa was not ruled by the African people themselves. Instead, many African countries were ruled by foreign governments from Britain, France, Germany, Portugal and Italy. Settlers from these faraway places moved to Africa and took land from the African people. Business people came, too. They built factories and mines, employed Africans to work in them and sent goods and profits out of Africa and back to Europe.

African people soon learned they could not stop what the powerful countries of Europe were doing. Worse still, the Europeans did not think they were doing wrong.

In 1912, six years before Rolihlahla Mandela was born, a new political party was founded in South Africa. It was called the African National Congress (ANC) and, like other parties elsewhere in Africa, it had a very strong message to spread amongst African people – the message of nationalism.

The ANC wanted to create a **multi-racial** South Africa, where black and white people could live side by side in peace and friendship. But, more importantly, the ANC was determined that South Africa should be ruled by Africans, not by the foreign governments of Europe.

Early members of the ANC, photographed in 1914.

His name is 'Nelson'

When Rolihlahla Mandela was five years old he was set to work as a herdboy, looking after sheep and cattle. Then, in 1925, when he was seven, he became the first person in his family ever to go to school. Rolihlahla's father wanted his son to do well in life, and he knew that a good education would help.

Rolihlahla was sent to a local **mission school**, run by Christian missionaries. On his first day there, his teacher told him that African names that were not Christian were not used at the school. He was given the English name

A reconstruction of the hut in which Nelson Mandela lived with the Thembu royal family.

'Nelson'. From that day on, Rolihlahla was known as Nelson Mandela.

In 1927, when Nelson was nine, his father died. It was a great shock to the young boy, and to his mother who was left to bring the family up on her own. To make things easier for her, Nelson went to live with the Thembu royal family, because the two families knew each other very well.

Chief Jongintaba Dalindyebo and his wife, NoEngland, lived in the Thembu capital of Mqhekezweni with their son, Justice. Nelson was accepted as part of the family.

Mandela's foster father, Chief Jongintaba Dalindyebo.

As Nelson grew up, he learned many things from Chief Jongintaba. He heard stories from long ago about brave Africans who had struggled to keep their land. They did not want foreign settlers from Europe to take it from them. Nelson heard how African leaders were arrested and sent to a prison far away on Robben Island. He never forgot these stories.

From boy to man

In 1934, Chief Jongintaba sent Mandela away to boarding school. Four years later, aged 20, he went to the University of Fort Hare, in the town of Alice.

At university, Mandela began to show he was a leader. He became involved in a protest about the poor food served to the students. Mandela was living up to his African name Rolihlahla, 'troublemaker'.

In 1940, Chief Jongintaba told Mandela he had chosen a bride for him. Mandela was not at all pleased and he ran away to Johannesburg, the capital city of South Africa.

The University of Fort Hare in Alice was a university for black African students only.

In Johannesburg, Mandela became a policeman at a gold mine. Chief Jongintaba found out where he was and told the mine owner to send him home. Mandela refused. He was determined to make his own way in the world.

Mandela decided he wanted to become a lawyer, and his cousin, Garlick Mbekeni, knew just the man to help him. He took him to meet Walter Sisulu, an influential African businessman with an office in Johannesburg. Sisulu was well-known for helping his fellow Africans. He found Mandela a job as a clerk at a law firm and the two men became good friends.

Mandela settled down to his new job. He was able to finish his studies at the University of Fort Hare by post, after which he became a student at the University of Witwatersrand, in Johannesburg. He studied law, and was the only black student in the department.

Walter Sisulu in the 1940s.

A divided country

In the 1940s, South Africa was a country divided by **racial discrimination**. It was a system called **apartheid**, meaning 'apartness'. Africans, Indians and all non-white people were kept apart from white people. The government was run by white people, and they found it easy to pass laws which favoured whites. It was a cruel, unfair system and non-white people hated it.

In 1942, Walter Sisulu encouraged Mandela to join the African National Congress (ANC) and attend their

Schoolgirls sit on benches marked 'for coloureds only'.

meetings. By doing this Mandela became involved in the politics of South Africa. He was young and full of energy, and he saw how the ANC could be used as a powerful force to fight for the rights of non-white people in South Africa, setting them free from racial discrimination.

Mandela made many friends in the ANC. These men decided that for the ANC to be taken seriously, it had to change the way it worked. So, in 1944 the ANC Youth League was formed, and Nelson Mandela was one of its founders. The Youth League leaders felt the ANC had not done enough to change the politics of South Africa. They wanted the ANC to become a mass movement of millions of ordinary people, all of whom wanted changes to be made to the system.

Children hand out ANC leaflets in the street.

Meetings of the Youth League were held at Walter Sisulu's house. It was a good place to talk about politics and make plans for the future.

The protests begin

Mandela's work with the ANC Youth League showed that he was a born leader, and he became an important person within it. Then, in 1948, the government of South Africa adopted the apartheid system as its official policy – they made it the law of the land.

The ANC knew it had to do something to speak out against the unfairness of 'apartness'. It announced its Programme of Action, in which it called for mass strikes, boycotts, protests and peaceful resistance – ideas thought up by the Youth League.

An ANC peaceful protest against apartheid, 1950s.

Instead of listening to the ANC, the government passed more new laws designed to put an end to the protests. Life for non-whites in South Africa became harder still, and the apartheid system was strictly enforced. It was forbidden for non-whites to marry white people. Many jobs could only be done by whites and there were separate public facilities for blacks and whites. Blacks were forbidden to live or work on land owned by whites and all black people were made to carry **'pass books'** which contained their photographs, fingerprints and details about where they were allowed to travel.

In protest against apartheid, Nelson Mandela burns his 'pass book'.

In 1952, the ANC called on the government to give non-whites the same rights as whites. The government refused. In reply, the ANC launched a peaceful, non-violent protest. It was called the Campaign for the Defiance of Unjust Laws. Mandela travelled the country encouraging people to defy the apartheid laws.

Mandela the leader

For his part in the Defiance Campaign, Mandela was arrested and brought to trial. But, because the protest had been peaceful, and no one had been hurt, Mandela was released without being sent to jail. However, he was banned from going to ANC meetings for two years and told not to leave Johannesburg for six months.

Mandela was leading a busier and busier life. In 1952, the same year as the Defiance Campaign, he started a law firm in Johannesburg with his friend, Oliver Tambo. It was

Oliver Tambo, photographed at the law firm he owned with Mandela.

the first law firm in South Africa owned and run by black Africans and it helped blacks who were suffering under the apartheid laws.

By stopping Mandela attending ANC meetings, the government of South Africa hoped to put an end to the protests against the apartheid system. Nothing could have been further from the truth. The ANC had become an important political organisation and, in 1952, Mandela became its deputy president.

In 1955, the ANC issued a list of principles known as the Freedom Charter. The Freedom Charter was the ANC's plan for the future of South Africa, looking forward to the day when racial discrimination came to an end.

Again, the government was outraged. In 1956, Mandela and 155 other ANC members were arrested. The government said the Freedom Charter showed that the ANC was a rebel organisation that wanted to take control of the country by force.

The 156 ANC members accused of treason in 1956.

Mandela and his colleagues were charged with treason. However, after a long trial, they were all found innocent.

Massacre at Sharpeville

On 21 March 1960, a protest against the apartheid laws was held at the town of Sharpeville. Things began peacefully, but as the crowd grew in size the police panicked and started shooting. Over 60 Africans were killed. Most of them were shot in the back as they tried to run from trouble.

The government of South Africa was criticised by many countries for the massacre at Sharpeville. In response, the government declared a **State of Emergency**, banned the ANC and arrested Mandela, along with many others. It was five months before Mandela was released.

Dead and wounded Africans lie in the streets, after the Sharpeville massacre.

The ANC organisation may have been banned, but it had thousands of supporters, not only in South Africa but all over the world. It was too big and too powerful to be stamped out by the government. Despite the ban, the leaders of the ANC vowed to continue their struggle against apartheid.

Members of the ANC faced being sent to prison for up to ten years. Mandela knew he had to

During his time in hiding, Mandela was nicknamed 'The **Black Pimpernel***'.*

carry on his work, but from now on it would be in secret. He grew a beard and dressed in different styles of clothing so that the police would not recognise him.

For years the ANC had been a peaceful, non-violent organisation – yet it had failed to bring an end to the apartheid system. Mandela, and the other ANC leaders, now began to think that violence might be the only way to defeat South Africa's cruel laws. It was agreed to form an army of fighters called Umkhonto we Sizwe, meaning 'Spear of the Nation'.

Prisoner number 466/64

In 1962, Mandela secretly left South Africa. He travelled to Ethiopia for a meeting with politicians from many African countries. He told them about the problems in his home country, and they promised to support the ANC in its struggle for freedom.

Mandela was abroad for several months. Besides visiting politicians, he made plans for members of Umkhonto we Sizwe, the ANC's secret army, to be trained.

On his return to South Africa, Mandela was arrested. He was charged with leaving the country illegally, and sentenced to five years in prison on Robben Island.

Mandela and other prisoners breaking stones in the prison yard.

Not long after he'd started this sentence, he was charged with a far more serious crime. Mandela, and the other leaders of Umkhonto we Sizwe, were accused of attempting to overthrow the government with violence. They were each sentenced to life in prison.

In 1964, Mandela started his life sentence in the maximum security prison on Robben Island, a few kilometres off the coast of South Africa. Mandela was prisoner number 466/64 (the prison's 466th prisoner of 1964).

Prison conditions were harsh. Food was poor, and Mandela's tiny cell was damp. He was made to do hard labour and could only have one visitor every six months. He was not even allowed to go to the funerals of his mother and eldest son.

Years after his release, Mandela visits his prison cell.

23

Mandela is released

In 1980, the ANC began a campaign to have Mandela released from prison. There was support from countries all over the world. Nelson Mandela had become the world's most famous prisoner.

In 1982, after eighteen years on Robben Island, Mandela was moved to Pollsmoor Prison, on the mainland of South Africa. Conditions were better there, and he was allowed to see his family more often. But outside prison, the apartheid system carried on as before.

During the 1980s there was widespread violence in many towns throughout South Africa. The ANC had become the mass movement that Mandela and its others leaders had hoped for, but at a price. Riots were common, property was damaged and people were attacked.

South African President F W de Klerk, who finally rejected the apartheid system and ordered Mandela's release in 1990.

Faced with mounting pressure from around the world, the government of South Africa, led by President F W de Klerk, began to hold secret talks with Mandela in 1986. They knew that if anyone could stop the violence, he could. Three years later, in 1989, the government released the other men who had gone to prison with Mandela. Things were starting to change for the better.

Mandela's own release came on 11 February 1990. He had spent 27 years in prison. It was late in the afternoon when Mandela walked through the prison gates to freedom. The world's press were waiting for him and pictures were televised live around the world. Mandela was then driven to Cape Town, where a crowd of 10,000 people were waiting for him at the City Hall. A banner hung from a balcony. It read: 'Nelson Mandela, the nation welcomes you home.'

Nelson Mandela and his wife, Winnie, punch the air victoriously as he is released.

President F W de Klerk also lifted the ban on the ANC and the ANC announced plans for a new South Africa, where non-whites and whites would be treated as equals.

President Nelson Mandela

Mandela's years in prison had not changed the things he believed in. He became the ANC leader, and held many meetings with President F W de Klerk to find a way of working together that would be good for whites and non-whites alike. Their partnership was recognised in 1993, when they were awarded the **Nobel Peace Prize.**

In April 1994, a general election was held in South Africa. For the first time in the country's history, men and woman of all races were allowed to vote.

There was little doubt which political party would win. Nelson Mandela led the ANC to victory, and became the

Nelson Mandela is sworn in as the new president of South Africa.

president of South Africa. A new era in history began and with it came the end of the hated apartheid system.

Mandela was president for five years. He was a living symbol of how a cruel and unfair system could be overturned. In 1999, at the age of 81, Mandela retired from politics to return to the Transkei. Today, he leads a quiet and simple life. In his long life he has never asked for much – Nelson Mandela is a man who has given everything he has to help others.

Nelson Mandela in his retirement, pictured with his third wife, Graca Machel.

Timeline

1918   *18 July:* Rolihlahla Dalibhunga Mandela is born.

1927   Mandela's father dies, and he goes to live with Chief Jongintaba Dalindyebo.

1939–40 Mandela goes to the University of Fort Hare.

1944   Mandela helps to form the ANC Youth League. He marries Evelyn Mase.

1948   The government brings in laws supporting racial discrimination (apartheid).

1952   The ANC launches the Campaign for the Defiance of Unjust Laws. Mandela is its Volunteer-in-Chief. Arrested and banned from ANC meetings for two years. Opens a law firm in Johannesburg. Becomes Deputy President of the ANC.

1956   Mandela goes on trial for treason.

1957   Mandela and his first wife Evelyn Mase are divorced.

1958   Mandela marries Winnie Madikizela.

1960   *21 March:* Sharpeville massacre, when 67 protesters are shot dead by the police. The ANC is banned. Mandela is arrested.

1961	Mandela forms 'Umkhonto we Sizwe'. Escapes the country and travels abroad.
1962	Mandela is jailed for five years.
1964	He is sentenced to life in prison.
1980	Pressure grows for the release of Mandela.
1986	Mandela begins talks with the government.
1989	Mandela meets President F W de Klerk.
1990	*11 February:* Mandela is set free after 27 years in prison.
1991	Mandela becomes president of the ANC.
1993	Mandela and President F W de Klerk are awarded the Nobel Peace Prize.
1994	Mandela becomes president of South Africa.
1996	Mandela and his second wife Winnie Madikizela are divorced.
1997	Mandela steps down as leader of the ANC.
1998	Mandela marries Graca Machel.
1999	Mandela retires from public life.
2005	Mandela's son dies from AIDS. Mandela spends much of his time campaigning against HIV/AIDS.

Glossary

apartheid A word meaning 'apartness'. It describes the policy of the government of South Africa from 1948 to 1994, in which non-whites were separated – kept apart – from whites.

Black Pimpernel Mandela was given this nickname by newspapers in the early 1960s, while he hid from the police. He was seen as an African version of the Scarlet Pimpernel, a character from fiction who also evaded capture.

mission school A school run by Christian missionaries.

multi-racial A society in which all people, regardless of their racial origins, are treated as equals.

nationalism A movement in which people strive towards governing their nation for themselves, rather than being ruled by people they regard as foreigners.

Nobel Peace Prize A prize awarded each year by the Norwegian Nobel Committee to a person (or persons) whose work has led to a more peaceful world.

pass books From 1952 to 1986 all black people in South Africa over the age of 16 had to carry an identity document, or pass book.

racial discrimination Where people are treated unfairly by others because of their racial origins. They are discriminated against.

State of Emergency Where a government takes extraordinary measures to keep control of the country, such as sending the army onto the streets to stop protests from happening.

Thembu A clan (tribe) of native Africans whose homeland is in the Transkei region of South Africa.

Transkei A region in South Africa, with its capital at Umtata.

Index